The Goddess

Who Forgot That She Was a Goddess

Written & Illustrated by Patricia Dines

Published by:
Community Action Publications
708 Gravenstein Hwy N, #104
Sebastopol, CA 95472
www.HealthyWorld.org/cap.html
Info@HealthyWorld.org

Library of Congress Control Number: 2015921339
ISBN: 978-0-9700941-4-8
Printed in China by Sunrise
Design & Printing Company
10 9 8 7 6 5 4 3 2 1
First Edition

1. Spirituality

2. Personal growth

3. Inspiration

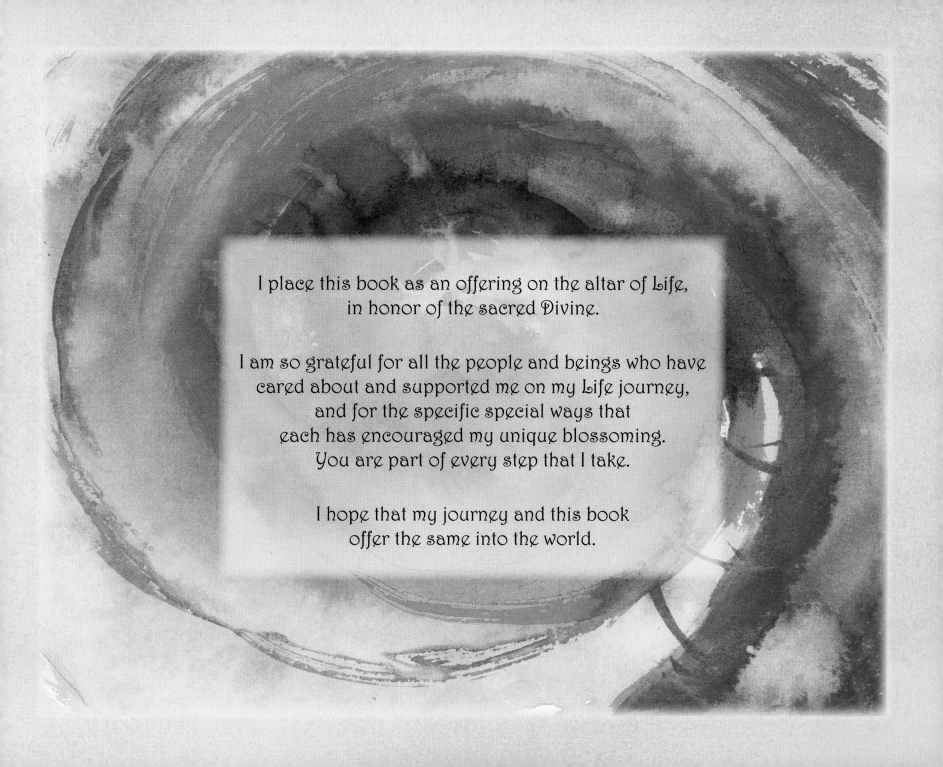

I place this book as an offering on the altar of Life,
in honor of the sacred Divine.

I am so grateful for all the people and beings who have
cared about and supported me on my Life journey,
and for the specific special ways that
each has encouraged my unique blossoming.
You are part of every step that I take.

I hope that my journey and this book
offer the same into the world.

Table of Contents

~~~~~~~~~~~~~~~~~~~~

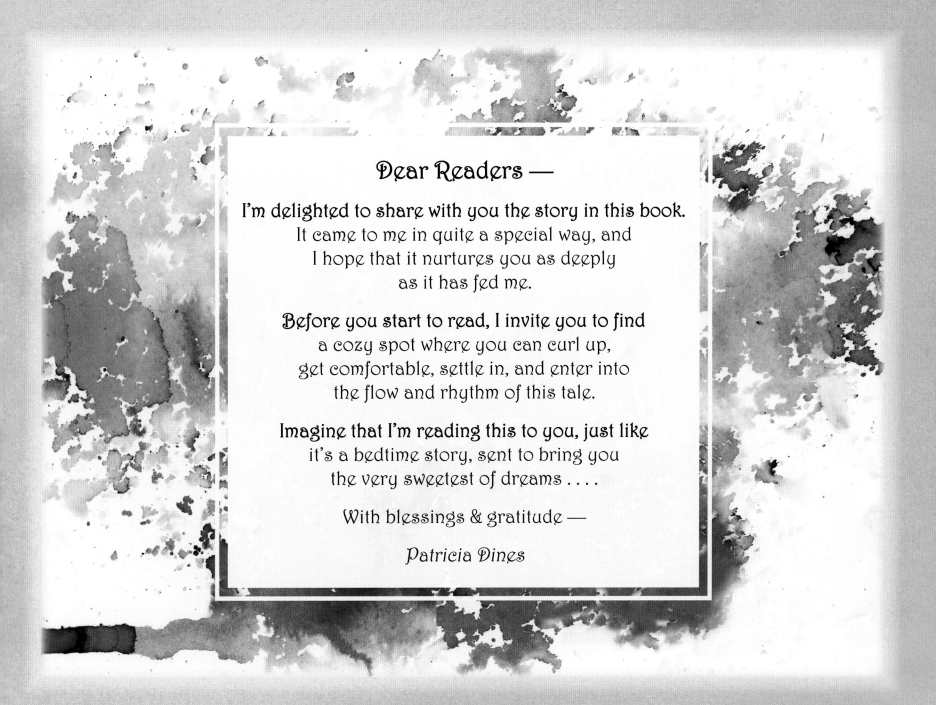

Dear Readers —

I'm delighted to share with you the story in this book.
It came to me in quite a special way, and
I hope that it nurtures you as deeply
as it has fed me.

Before you start to read, I invite you to find
a cozy spot where you can curl up,
get comfortable, settle in, and enter into
the flow and rhythm of this tale.

Imagine that I'm reading this to you, just like
it's a bedtime story, sent to bring you
the very sweetest of dreams . . . .

With blessings & gratitude —

Patricia Dines

O nce upon a time there was a goddess who forgot that she was a goddess.

(I mean, who could forget such a thing? But she did!)

This goddess lived high up on a hill, all alone.

Around her house there were birds flying, and ribbons in the air, colored bright white and beaming yellow and rich dark blue, all sparkling with the sun.

It was all very beautiful.

But she couldn't see that. Because there was a great big teardrop on this goddess' heart, and that's all that she could see, this big teardrop, wherever she looked.

(How very sad, right?)

But one day, on a day that seemed just like any other, the goddess heard a voice inside herself suggest that she go down the hill and into the forest. She had felt this voice resonate within her before, and trusted it, but it had never given her this type of message before.

It also showed her, in her mind's eye, an image of where she was to go. She was surprised at how beautiful it was.

The ground there was all covered with a deep, thick, soft green moss. On top of it were sprinkled countless little bright white and yellow flowers, sparkling just like fairies' laughter.

All around stood big tall trees, trees as old as time, peaceful, not needing or reaching for anything, just happy to be standing tall and sure in this place.

Beams of sunlight filtered down through the leaves, making soft sweet patterns on the moss.

Every once in a while, a butterfly would appear in a beam of light, suddenly revealed in all its beautiful colors — just for a moment — and then it would disappear again.

The goddess sighed seeing this blissful imagined scene, but then she felt impatient.

Crisply, she said back to the voice, "OK, that's beautiful and all that.
But why on earth should I go to the trouble of going there? I'm quite comfortable here!"

The voice seemed to smile as it soothingly replied, "Ah, but if you go, the moss there will heal the sadness in your heart.

"I know that your sadness brings you great pain. But in it I also see your beauty.

"You are sad because your heart is as big as everything.

"Your sadness and your beauty are the same."

Hearing this, the goddess felt an energy move inside her, quiet and sweet.

So she relented and said, "OK, it does seem that it would feel good to be there in the forest."

To try out the idea, she walked to her front door, opened it, and stepped outside. She felt the cool air all around her.

But then she stopped and spoke to the voice.

"I do have a question, though. What should I wear? I don't know what to wear to be in the forest."

Now it was the voice's turn to be impatient. "Are you kidding?" it replied. "You want to know what to wear?!"

The goddess knew that the question sounded silly. So she paused and looked inside herself. Still, she saw that that was her question.

"Yes," she said firmly, "That's what I want to know."

As soon as the goddess said that, suddenly, birds came all around her. They took the ribbons that were floating in the air — these ribbons that were half of the material realm and half of the spirit realm — and used them to weave an amazing dress all around her.

This dress was more beautiful than any that had ever been seen before, made of all the essential things of the world — the amazing colors and species and loves and deep yearnings — all of these were being woven into this dress.

As she saw the dress emerging around her, the goddess felt her body relax and shift at its very core.

She smiled and knew that she was now ready to head out on this mysterious adventure.

So she looked around until she saw the top of the trail that she knew she was to take. She paused, wondering why she'd never noticed it before. Then she stepped into its opening, and followed as it turned sharply downhill into a series of rough and rocky turns. Finally, she reached a small flat area and saw that she was at the edge of a thick dark forest.

And then — she went in. She wasn't sure where to go next, so she just followed what felt right. As she walked around trees and rocks, she felt the soft dirt under her feet, heard the gentle crunch of pine needles, and was filled by the beauty of the forest around her.

Then suddenly, after she went around a bend, she was amazed to see the place that the voice had shown her. Yes, here it was, with the deep, thick, soft green moss sprinkled with flowers made of fairies' laughter, the tall rooted trees, and the butterflies dancing with the sunbeams.

The moss looked so soft and comfortable to her, so welcoming, that she decided to lie down here — gently, carefully, so as not to hurt its aliveness.

As she settled in and started to relax, she felt slowly rising beneath her, around her, the sweetest of energies — a feeling of totally pure caring and honoring and support — like all the love of the universe was creating this soft bed just to soothe her.

Without knowing why, she felt tears start to come up, softly, from the center of her being. Soon, her whole body was crying and shaking, filled with an unnamed pain. All of her became these tears.

As she cried, images crossed her mind. Images of those who had hurt her and those she had hurt. Images of all the beings in the world who had done harm to others, and those who had been harmed by them.

She cried seeing all this pain. Then she cried at what she saw so clearly underneath it — the profound beauty designed into every single person's heart — and the sadness when that beauty was lost, when beings were less than they wanted to be, or could be, in their magical divine design.

Then she cried because she knew deeply that there was no difference between her heart and any other, all yearning for the same things, and crying for what was not.

And then she cried because she hadn't known how much she needed to cry, or that it would feel so good.

And all around her was the moss, and the tears that poured out of her mingled with its softness, and fed it deeply. They all became one, nestled inside infinity.

And then the tears were done and she became quiet again.

She heard the birds rustling and making preparations with each other. She watched a family of deer move through the woods. She saw the beams of sunlight, lower now, but still filtering through the leaves and scattering light crystals all around. She felt her breath move gently in and out of her body, and the muscles in her face relax.

As a happy sigh escaped from her body, she noticed that it sounded just like the stream flowing at the bottom of the hill, quietly nourishing and cleansing everything there.

The blood running in her body felt just like that water, sweet and calm and pure.

She was at peace.

But then after a while she stirred and realized that she was starting to feel lonely, that she wanted to share this experience with other humans.

She wondered if the voice that had spoken to her could appear as a person, or if other people could come here. So she asked this of the voice.

And the voice replied, "This place is just for you. But there is a place near here for you to invite people.

"When you want to invite them, go to that place and be in your heart, and they will come."

"Really?!" the goddess said, feeling skeptical. "I don't know, that seems a little, um ... unrealistic. Are you really saying that all I need to do is send out some kind of psychic heart-o-gram and people will just come, that's all? I find that hard to believe."

The voice sighed and patiently said, "Yes, that's all you need to do. They will come. They're just waiting for your signal."

The goddess looked down and quietly said, "But why would they come to me on just the basis of some psychic vibe?

"There are so many people on this earth who are much more lovable than me, much easier to love, much more worthy of love, not horribly flawed like I am.

"I really think that people would go to those other people long before they would come to me."

The voice replied gently, sweetly, tenderly, "Look again. Is that really true?

"Is that who you are, in your heart or your actions? Is that really how you've been with people or moved through this world?

"Of all the beings on this planet, are you really the one who doesn't deserve any love at all?

"What would you say if someone else said that about themself? Perhaps that *all* beings deserve love?

"Why can you see that about everyone else, but not yourself?

"What if your heart were big enough to include you ... ?"

The goddess looked up and felt the filtered light gently touching her face. As she considered what the voice had said, something shifted inside her center.

"Thank you," she said softly. "Yes, I see now that I am just as precious as all the other beings in this world. How beautiful it is that each of us always has this magical divine essence at our core — even when we're struggling or unsure or in pain or trying to figure out how to walk our mysterious journey on this planet. Still, we are divine."

As she said this, a door opened inside her. Out of it came a part of her that she didn't even know was there. All on its own, an energy of movement and delight filled her body, became it, and she started to dance, a silly impish dance — like she was a prankster and a trickster and a child just delighting in life. She felt free and playful in a way that would bring a smile to any heart that could see.

And, as the goddess let herself dance and spin around, simply go for the ride, she laughed, just for the joy of it.

"I see!" she said to the voice, "My feelings of unworthiness blocked my joy.

"My unworthiness was just joy in a box!

"But there's no need for me to hide my core self in shame, for it is beauty and beloved.

"Please help me remember not to close that box again, and to let my joy dance free."

She could feel the hum all around her saying, "Of course."

Then the goddess felt ready to go to the place that was for inviting friends. She saw in her mind which way to go, and started walking.

As she went along, she was amazed by all the delightful sights and sounds of the forest. Then suddenly she found herself in a clearing filled with warm bright light. The plants here were so lush, with a glow that seemed to come from being fed very deeply.

"Yes, this must be the place," she thought.

She sat down in the center of the clearing, and got comfortable. Then, as the voice had described, she focused on feeling the love in her heart and letting it beam from her.

It started as a tiny soft pink hum in her center. Soon she felt it filling every cell in her body, healing and softening every wound and doubt and awkwardness inside her, resonating all around her.

She felt like a child being cuddled in the eternal mother's soft pink blanket.

And then, just as the voice had said would happen, she saw other people enter the clearing from different parts of the forest. And, to her surprise, they walked right towards her!

She knew some of the people, and didn't know others. But she could see their divinity shining in their broad smiles and pink glows.

The goddess stood up, said hello, and hugged each one. They delighted in doing the same with each other.

Then these divine ones all sat down in a circle. One by one, each person described their unique journey to get here. They revealed the passions that had driven them, the difficulties that had challenged them, the disappointments they had overcome, and the dreams they now carried.

As each person spoke, everyone else in the circle listened deeply, holding their hearts open and seeking to see and honor the unique beauty in each being before them.

Each of these offerings were made simply. But, from their unique and sacred threads, these divine ones created a beautiful fabric of connection and relationship — and a safe and nurturing space for all.

And, through this, the shared pink light grew.

Every once in a while, someone would pause to savor the beauty of it all, murmuring their gratitudes to the wise inner voices, and feeling awe at the opportunity to experience life's extravagant divine design.

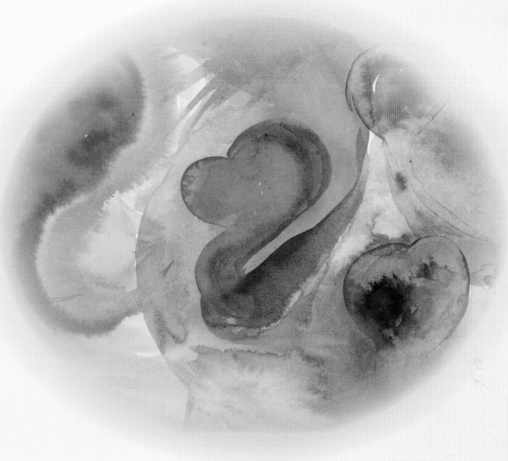

And, from time to time, these divine ones would leave this lush, light-filled clearing — perhaps to return to their personal spots, or to do the more ordinary activities of their everyday lives.

Still, wherever each of them went, they knew that they could always come back here, to connect with and nurture the shared heart space of the divine.

One day the goddess was walking in this part of the woods with one of her new goddess friends, and her friend asked, "So, how do you feel now?"

And she looked inside herself and smiled as she answered simply,

"I am happy just being the goddess that I am."

~ The End ~

Beyond the Story

So I hope that you've enjoyed this story.
I invite you to just sit with it for a bit.

After that, if you want, this section offers some
"behind the scenes" for you to explore.

Answering Reader Questions

What do you mean by a goddess?

A common question I get is about the meaning of the term goddess in this story. The short answer is: A divine female woman. Which all women are. Or the divine core in each woman. Or the divine female energy within all of us.

In this culture, the gods and goddesses are usually seen as separate and perfect, shimmering bright in stark contrast to our flawed human flesh and bone. However, what I've been shown on my spiritual path is that we are all divine at the core, i.e. we all have an inner god and goddess, and our job is to discover and seek to manifest that beauty in ourselves and our lives.

Thus, the external deities aren't separate from us but part of us and a model that we can seek to emulate. Even when our expressions are imperfect (by whatever standard one uses), our core self is divine, and we can keep aligning ourselves to that.

I like this approach, because it allows me to feel peaceful in my center while continuing to grow according to my beautiful internal design.

Who is the voice?

Well, I encourage everyone to experience it in their own way. My approach isn't part of any particular religious tradition and can fit with many or none.

For me, the voice is perhaps intuition, inner wisdom, or the divine spirit. One of the messages I hear in this story is the value of developing a direct and clear connection to our authentic intuition, and trusting what it shows us.

Of course, we need to be careful that we're listening to inner wisdom and not fears, prejudices, projections, unconsidered impulses, etc. It's key to learn how to tell the difference.

For me, part of how I know it's the divine voice is that it shows me the beauty in myself and how to express it. It supports me in nurturing that in others. It never wants me to harm anyone, and helps me make wise choices that feel good and true to my core.

More Fun with the Goddess: Book Activity Ideas

Here are some further ways that you can connect with the ideas and feelings of this book — to nurture yourself and deepen your journey with this divine tale.

• Put the book by your bed and read it before you go to sleep. This sets you up for sweet dreams and offers a chance to integrate your experiences of this into your dreams and life.

• Journal or draw what you experienced with this book, to bring it deeper into yourself. What did it bring up in you? How do you relate to your intuition and core divine self? How is that blocked and how would you like it to flow?

• Get to know the female deities or saints in your spiritual path or other ones. Doing this can help us see and manifest our own beautiful divine core. For instance, I personally love Quan Yin, Goddess (Bodhisatva) of Compassion. Her compassion heals and feeds the heart.

• Consider other ways to nurture your heart. Here are a few simple ideas you might want to try: Spray some diluted pure lavender essential oil on your sheets, or put a piece of rose quartz by your bed. Or get a rose quartz necklace to wear over your heart. Maybe put lemon balm (stalks or dried herb) in a water pitcher in the fridge, for a healthy refreshing beverage. Or plant some lavender or lemon balm, and smell them deeply, to get to know the plants and integrate them into your life.

• For more information related to this theme, and to continue the conversation, see www.HealthyWorld.org/GoddessBook.

• If you enjoyed the art, some pieces are available as greeting cards and quality wall art. The website has more information.

You might also have fun sharing this book with others, and supporting its way in the world. For instance, you could:

• Read this book to others, individually or in groups, including children and women in need. Maybe ask someone to read it to you. The experience feels wonderful in both directions!

• Recommend this book to friends, and post your praise on Facebook, Amazon, book review websites, and other media.

• Give a copy of this book to a friend, women's shelter, spiritual library, or other place where you think it could serve others. Pass along the empowering nourishment!

• Suggest that your local bookstore or library carry this book.

• Encourage your local newspaper or magazine to review it.

• Invite me to read excerpts of this book at a book signing, or the whole book for a gathering.

• Write me and tell me your experience of the story!

About the Author & Illustrator, Patricia Dines

There are many threads in my life that bring me to this moment and offering this book.

On the practical side, I bring the skills and experiences I've gleaned from over 30 years as a professional writer, graphic artist, public speaker, and community educator. During this time, I've written and presented a wide range of books, newsletters, articles, reports, essays, classes, training materials, client projects, and more.

About 20 years ago, because of my love for the sacred earth, I started to specialize in environmental and community issues. My vision was to skip the too-common fear-and-shame approach to this topic. Instead, I've sought to inspire and empower all of us (including myself!) to reclaim our collective power for creating a joyful future and world. (If you want to learn more about my work in that realm, see *www.PatriciaDines.info* and *www. AskEcoGirl.info*, which include links to my Facebook pages.)

But the roots of this book go deeper than my professional path — into my childhood, my personal

growth journey, and my precious relationship with the divine. I didn't have a name for the life force when I was growing up. But, looking back, I know that I felt it when I entered into the dimensional playground of nature, and became immersed in its nurturing wise beauty. I also know that it's been present when I've felt the call to write down mystical pieces such as this one — these expressions that emerge in a different style than my more practical writing and have been such a lifeline of sanity for me.

I am so grateful that the divine has been with me as I've walked through my life and sought to shape myself and my path. What a blessing!

For so long, my goal has been just to be its ambassador on this planet, to express and embody in some way the beauty that I've experienced with it.

So the story in this book is just one of so many gifts that I've received in my relationship with the divine. I'm deeply honored to be the carrier of this tale. I hope that it reminds you of your own core divinity and brings you a luscious taste of the sacred eternal.

In gratitude —

Patricia

The Source of This Tale

For those who want to know the backstory ... this tale came to me on October 25, 1998, in a very special and magical way.

I was at my first Bioneers Conference, at San Francisco's Fort Mason Center. This innovative event was created from the realization that folks in various fields were working on different aspects of environmental and social change, but often didn't know about each other. The Bioneers' vision was to connect us with this wider conversation, multiplying all of our efforts.

So I was delighted to be listening to these amazing speakers, powerfully illuminating issues that deeply matter to me.

But my body started feeling quite uncomfortable, and I didn't know what it needed. I wanted to keep listening to the talks, so I tried lying down in the back of the room, but that didn't help. Neither did quietly pacing there.

I started worrying. Did I need to go to a doctor? I decided to go outside to see if that helped, or, if not, to go for aid.

As I hurried out the door, an ally (Siggy) was coming in. She said "Hi," and I replied in kind, but kept rushing out. To my surprise, she caught up with me and asked, "Are you mad at me?" I turned to look at her and said, "Oh no, not at all. I just don't feel very well."

She nodded and said, "Yes, it is intense in there." I burst into an *Aha!* laugh. That was it! I'm an emotional intuitive in a room full of powerful, intelligent, caring people who are engaged in important and passionate global work. There's probably more energy running through that room than in most places!

Still, I needed to find my center again. So I asked her to help me work with these energies. I was delighted when she said yes.

So we found a nearby lawn, and I invited her to sit down. I stayed standing and went into a body movement that I do to center myself. That technique is a story in itself, but basically I softly bend my knees like I'm slightly sitting in an invisible chair, then slowly shift the energy inside my legs from side to side, like sands shifting back and forth. As I get fully present with my body's energies, I let them lead the way.

This process usually generates intuitive movement that helps me release and connect with my body's wisdom. But this time I was totally surprised when I spoke instead — and the first line of this story came out. How wonderful!

Both Siggy and I were enchanted by it, and curious what would happen next. So I kept moving with my body's wisdom, and another line came out, then another, until the basics of this story came through, to both of our delights. I am so grateful to Siggy for holding safe space in support of this story being born. (I also appreciate the fertile atmosphere of Bioneers!)

After it was done, I felt such an amazing clearing and healing in my body, and we were both in awe of what had just happened. I said to her, "I think I should go write that down," and she replied, "Oh yeah!" I did, and gave her a copy. Over the years I've enhanced this, until it's become the tale you read here.

This experience has long been a treasure for me, so I'm thrilled to have finally shaped it into this book. I hope that it nurtures you on your divine journey as well.

About the Artwork

The journey of creating the artwork for this book has also been very powerful for me. For years, I knew that I wanted to do an illustrated version of this story, but wasn't sure how to approach it. Should I draw the pictures myself? Or hire someone? I explored these options, but they didn't come together, and I had lots of other projects on my plate.

But then one day I decided to go through my old artwork, to see if I could find pieces for this book.

I've done intuitive paintings and drawings for years, but they were just for my own personal pleasure and process, so I was skeptical that I'd have enough to fit this tale.

But, to my amazement, I kept finding ones that I felt matched perfectly. When I found the one of the goddess on the hill (page 5), it seemed as if I'd painted it just for those words. Wow!

That's when I felt that I actually could illustrate this book myself. That was such an empowering expansion of my knowing of myself, and a continued gift to me of this process. I loved that the pictures would reflect my style along with the words.

So I scanned my candidate pieces. They all started on paper, made with watercolor paint, art markers, colored pencils, and black drawing pencils. Then I pulled out excerpts, added elements, adjusted content, and made montages, until I had just the feeling I wanted for each page. My vision was that readers would experience each page as a moment, complete and enriching

in itself, with the words and artwork coming together as one. It's been so thrilling for me to watch that process happen.

I also love that each art piece came from, and expresses, a unique divine moment. That inspiration, plus the range of media and styles, gives the book a suggestive dream-like quality that I think aligns well with its theme.

For a while, though, I was stumped about what to put on the cover. Then I remembered a life vision painting I'd done for myself. I dug it out, scanned it in, trimmed it up, and was amazed at how well it expresses the character of this book!

There were also a few elements that came to me via serendipity. One day I was at the Open Studio of a local artist (Diane Luiz) and saw an area she'd set up for visitors to try some crystal watercolors. Nearby were the small doodle discards of various people who'd come during the day. I felt that some of these pieces would work well in this book, so I asked her permission to use them. She cheerfully granted it. Since the authorship of these pieces is unknown, I can only credit and appreciate them and her as part of this book's magical process! (They are the backgrounds on pages 1, 17, and 27, plus the tree on page 15.)

I hope that describing my experience helps you connect more with the artwork here. I also hope that it encourages you to nurture your own creativity, in whatever way inspires you. You never know what you might find!

Ordering Information

The Goddess makes a great gift! Plus, quantity discounts and wholesale pricing are available.

For more information:

www.HealthyWorld.org/GoddessBook

Community Action Publications
708 Gravenstein Hwy N, #104
Sebastopol, CA 95472

Thank you for your interest in *The Goddess*!